CW01626722

’s Experience of Pastoral Care

What (Really) Promotes Clergy Well-being?

Sean Cathie

Independent Scholar

GROVE BOOKS LIMITED

RIDLEY HALL RD CAMBRIDGE CB3 9HU

Contents

Acknowledgments

The starting point for this book was the small empirical research project I did as part of my doctorate. Doing that within the King's doctoral was intellectually stimulating and enriching. I am grateful to all who taught on that course and especially to James Steven for helping me to articulate what I really wanted to study and Geoffrey Court for his encouragement, patience and understanding support; to my clergy cell group: Peter Cotton, Keith Jones, David Parry and Julian Reindorp, including those who have died over the years, John Garton, Graham Shaw and Alan Wolstencroft. Stimulating and interesting conversations with too many others to name aided me in my quest to make sense of the puzzle of experience. Finally, a special thanks to my wife Elizabeth for her care and support which has made writing this possible.

The cover image is copyright © Grove Books Ltd

Copyright © Sean Cathie 2024

First Impression June 2024
ISSN 0144-171X
ISBN 978 1 78827 395 4

1 Introduction

Why We Need to Talk about Clergy Well-being

Acknowledging the Reality of Clergy Stress

'The hardest work I've ever done, and the most stressful, was as a parish priest—mainly because it was isolated, insatiably demanding and I was on the whole working without close colleagues—and that wears people down.' With these words, Archbishop Justin opened a milestone debate in General Synod in July 2017.[1] Having the Archbishop of Canterbury testify to the reality of the stress of ministry was a significant and powerful moment in the life of the Church. Especially as he had previously worked in the 'real world' as an executive with an oil company and this had included negotiating with terrorists which, he had warned his wife, could lead to his death. For him to open that debate with that personal testimony had great significance for parish clergy. It gave the stress of ministry a recognition that it had not had before. More formal recognition was later given when General Synod adopted the *Covenant on Clergy Care and Well-being*.[2] Since then dioceses have been responding to the *Covenant* and the practice of reflective practice groups and the importance of self-care have entered into the language of clergy well-being.

Significant levels of stress remain

However, the ongoing *Living Ministry* research and the surveys that *The Times* and the Unite union conducted in 2023 suggest that significant levels of stress remain.[3] This is underlined by recent work on why ordinand numbers have fallen 38% since 2020. Staff involved at diocesan and training level identified clergy well-being as the first most influential factor.[4] In addition, a well-informed account of distrust within the Church, *Trust and Trustworthiness within the Church of England*, has recently enlarged our understanding of the sources of distrust within the Church. Whilst its concern is with the Church as a whole, it is highly relevant to the issue of the stress of ministry and the need to think systemically about it. I shall reference it when appropriate.[5] It demonstrates why we need to think outside the box of the counselling model and consider the question raised by Dr Liz Graveling when she presented one report on the *Living Ministry* research. How, she asked, can the kindness of individual pastoral relationships be translated into our organizational life?[6]

The *Trust* report is an invaluable guide to thinking about this question. It reinforces the argument for organizational ways of responding to the stress of ministry with its account of the grave ill-being of the institution of the Church. It is a valuable resource for understanding the sources of clergy ill-being and its account of the spirituality of trust is vital for enabling more effective pastoral care throughout the Church and for addressing the spiritual needs of those outside the Church.[7] In short, exploring the stress of ministry in relation to the spirituality of trust leads us to a deeper understanding of the task and opportunities for ministry in our time. However, whilst this book aims to be comprehensive in scope, it is not possible to be so in detail.

Travelling Through the Landscape of Ministry

I undertook my research into *The Clergy's Experience of Pastoral Care* using an interdisciplinary approach. Three complementary concerns provided the organizing focus. These were first, the clergy's experience of pastoral care, secondly, the stress of ministry and thirdly, the Church's own practice of pastoral care. This last point of the triangle answers the need for a distinctively Christian or a theological and spiritual response. This is distilled as the essential task that I shall present in the last two chapters. To explore these concerns, I drew on theology, sociology and social applications of psychoanalysis to provide a multidimensional view of clergy well-being.

The Ecology of Pastoral Care

Taking this journey through the landscape of ministry reveals the ecology of pastoral care. Grounded in the community and worshipping life of the Church, at its best such an ecology 'enables people and communities to love God and each other better.'[8] The significance of this is brought out by one theologian reflecting on his experience of the L'Arche communities. Here 'helpers and handicapped are tested to their limits, and it is clear that for gentleness to survive it has to be sustained by a whole ecology of beliefs, practices and supports.'[9] Because caring activities need much more than the specific skills, such as counselling and reflective practice, that enable the many activities which teach people and communities to love God and each other better. Ranging as they do from choirs to youth clubs and more, this comment reminds us that, for these activities to retain their pastoral character, they need an ecology that weaves the relationships and activities together with beliefs and practices. In human society, this is what the term 'culture' describes.

Like the natural environment, the life and culture of the Church has suffered from disruptions of many kinds. To focus on clergy well-being, without considering these, screens out the effects of these disruptions of the Church's social, cultural and relational ecology. In other words, to promote clergy well-being requires that we take account of beliefs and practices that undergird and direct pastoral care. To understand clergy ill-being, we need to take account not only of the Church's damaged social ecology but also of how this is true of the world beyond the Church, the wider society in which we live. For without question, that is exhibiting many signs of stress and strain, too. One of the most telling symptoms is the failure to reform the provision of social care and the neglect of mental health services, especially for young people, to name just some. Care as a principle seems to have a very low priority.

This changed and damaged ecology, I suggest, is the context and generator of the stresses of ministry today. For the Church and its ministers, it is linked to the decline of worshipping members and the increase of those who self-identify as having no religion. This widening gap between Christian believers and the rest of society is a significant challenge and raises big questions. The links between church and society no longer work as supportively as they once did. There is, then, a social and systemic dimension to the stress of ministry, reflecting the social and cultural context in which ministry is exercised. There is also the context of the Church itself as organization.

The phenomenon of clergy stress is more accurately described as the stress of ministry

The first insight from an ecological perspective is that the phenomenon and experience of clergy stress is more accurately described as the stress of *ministry*. This takes our focus from the individual to the occupation and its setting. This change of emphasis is vital for a more accurate understanding of what undermines clergy well-being. It identifies the significant factor as 'the *what* not the *who*.'[10] Naming the occupational sources of stress is what Archbishop Justin did in his speech. This frees those who experience it from its associations of personal weakness and failure and directs our gaze to those shared sources of stress in the work which affect everyone in ministry and, in truth, everyone of faith. This dignifies the clergy's experience with a more accurate identification and discourages the tendency to scapegoat those showing symptoms of such stress.

The Questions this Raises

The widening gap between Christian believers and the rest of society raises big questions and strains the resources of the Church on many fronts, from maintaining the parish system to speaking persuasively and credibly to non-believers.[11] These pressures affect the Church as a whole and we may also guess that their effect on our senior clergy is as great, if not greater, as on frontline clergy. The *Trust* report suggests these are also sources of the distrust. Understanding them in relation to the stress of ministry, then, matters.

In particular, two strategic issues can be discerned behind the symptoms of the stress of ministry. The first is a question of meaning: 'What is the Church for?' This lurks behind the fact that modern society sees no need for it and that current provision for the clergy is failing.[12] The second is an organizational issue. When a significant proportion of clergy are overcome by the pressures and unable to minister well, this is a terrible waste of clergy talent.[13] There is both a missional and a pastoral imperative for developing more effective provision. Doing so has the potential to improve the Church's effectiveness more widely. Seeing the stress of ministry as the symptom that we need to understand opens up this more comprehensive perspective. This is a version of systems thinking which focuses on the relationship and connections *between* different parts of the system, such as between frontline clergy and senior clergy or between the Church and society. Identifying these vulnerable interconnections is what the *Trust* report does and indicates how interventions at such points could address the pervasive distrust and resulting poor organizational functioning. The key for doing this is in that principle of pastoral care of facing both ways, here between, say, the centre and the frontline, and between the pastoral and the managerial.

Insights for Pastoral Care of Ecclesial Communities

Furthermore, learning about the pastoral care of the clergy yields valuable insights for the pastoral care of congregations. But, you may ask, can the pastoral care of clergy really be relevant to that of congregations? Their experiences and roles are so different. They are and they are not. First, the benefit of starting with the clergy's experience is that what is needed pastorally, but is missing in practice, is identified from the clergy's own experience and so is made visible. If we can address that fruitfully, then the lessons learned will be applicable to the pastoral care of congregations. Secondly, both pastoral care of the clergy and of congregations suffers from the blinkering dominance of the secular counselling model of one-to-one support. The more comprehensive and ecological framework of pastoral care in the Christian tradition, that I have sketched here, can widen our vision and enable us to respond more effectively to clergy ill-being, repair the distrust and renew pastoral care within congregations too.

Questions for Reflection

- How does thinking of pastoral care as an ecology change your understanding of it?
- Where, in your situation, are the holes in this web of care relations?
- For office holders, both lay and ordained: what sources of stress do you experience in connection with your role?

2 The Weakness of Current Provision

How the Individual Focus Screens Out Key Sources

In the last chapter, I argued that the stress of ministry needs to be understood in more comprehensive terms. Enlarging our view highlights three dimensions that are missed by the individual focus. These are: the Church's own traditions of pastoral care, stress at work in organizational and occupational terms and, finally, the social-historical contextual dimension of ministry today.

The Church's Traditions of Pastoral Care

Stephen Pattison made the point over thirty years ago that contemporary pastoral practice has shrunk compared to that of the past. Pastoral responses are now dominated by the secular, therapeutic model of one-to-one counselling and it is assumed that good pastoral support must be on that basis.[14] This assumption blocks creative thinking and awareness of other approaches which are necessary for two reasons. Practically, support cannot be given to everyone on that individual basis. The way forward is to begin with the community. Both theological and ecological understandings converge by seeing the individual as a member of the community and the life of the community as the primary means of pastoral care (1 Thess 4.18; 5.12–19, 14). It is significant that Jesus' Parable of the Lost Sheep concludes with the lost being brought back to the flock (Matt 18.10–14). But a different loss, of a living connection with our tradition, means our vision and practice of pastoral care has been uncritically shaped by contemporary secular norms.[15]

What is particularly missing is an appreciation of the mediating role of ministry in all its forms, straddling the boundary between God and the world so that 'people and communities may love God and each other better.'[16] Integral to this are the tasks of oversight and teaching, particularly interpreting the presenting situation in relation to God. These address the two strategic issues raised in the last chapter and are very much needed by clergy feeling drained by the demands of ministry.[17] The anxiety this generates is contained and made more bearable when it can be addressed and discussed. At present, this mostly happens outside the Church's organizational life and appropriately so. However, such reflective spaces should not be limited to clergy reflecting privately on their pastoral practice. The *Trust* report points to the need for improved communication across the various organizational boundaries.

One way to assist this would be by providing safe reflective spaces that span the boundaries where suspicion and distrust are present. When the fruits of such reflection are brought into acts of worship, there is the opportunity for the concerns to be brought into 'the relational dynamics of the holiness of God.' Then, through the resulting transformation, it loses its shame and powerlessness and can lead 'to active connection with, and embodiment of holiness in, the multiple aspects of the wider world.'[18] Such pastoral care has limitless effects.

The Consensus on Stress at Work

Archbishop Justin said how stressful it was being a parish priest. Authorities from the world of work go further and describe chronic stress as destructive. From their investigations, they have concluded that stress at work is better understood as occupational and that organizational approaches are needed to address it. The best way is 'an integrated, organizational strategy' so that, instead of being an add-on activity, it becomes 'the way we do things around here.' Both management and employees object to this. The former often see it as inconvenient and not part of the business while the employees often view the actions of senior management with suspicion.[19]

Nonetheless, organizational self-interest supports the strategic organizational approach because it results in companies' performance greatly improving, as well as the health of employees. 'There's a famous study by Alex Edmans at the London Business School, which takes the 100 best places to work in the US and their evaluation, compared with the rest of the top companies, and tracks it over 25 years. And the top best places to work increase their share value 50 percent relative to the others.'[20] Similarly, *The Sunday Times* survey of the best companies to work for in the UK reported that they have a 13 per cent lower staff turnover (half the UK average) and consistently outperform the FTSE 100 companies. The reasons for this were that benefits flowed into improvements in employee engagement as well as with well-being, line-management and team working.[21] Addressing the system as a whole rather than as a series of individual problems is what makes such a difference. I turn now to the third dimension of the stress of ministry.

The Social and Historical Context for Ministry Today

The context for ministry today is marked by accumulated disruptions to the ecology of relations between Church and society. This is a key source of strain for the institution and its ministers. By disruptions I refer to the ending of Christendom when 'Western European society and culture was formed within the Christian framework.' This gave society a moral vision grounded in a 'transcendental order' with its sense of being part of 'a moral universe in which both personal and social acts were evaluated.'[22] This was grounded, however, in a religious sense that 'articulated the culture's deepest aspirations.'[23] We are aware that Christendom, that medieval unity of church and society, has ended. However, we do not appreciate how this has affected the Church by 'robb(ing it) of much of its former social, political and cultural significance.' *This* is why the Church is seen as 'marginal' to 'the mainstream concerns of ordinary people' and therefore 'as anachronistic.' Some remnants of that vision of Church and society and its transcendental order remain but for most of our secular contemporaries, the Church hardly figures as a source of meaning. As 'the representative figure of the Church, the clergyman feels in his own person the frustrations and dilemmas that result' without realizing how deeply rooted this cultural gap is and without knowing how to make sense of it.[24]

Aspects of this medieval social partnership persist in certain niches within the wider ecology, for example, between some Church-based schools and Oxbridge colleges where continuities between them foster the carrying forward of Christian faith and practice.

Questions for Reflection

- Are you aware of a gap between your community of faith and the rest of society? If so, how does it affect you? If not, why is that?
- Do you agree that the Church institution shows signs of 'grave ill-being'? How do you make sense of these?
- Are the pressures your community faces talked and prayed about?
- For office holders: do you feel supported in fulfilling your role?

3 Understanding the Stress of Ministry

Contextual and Occupational Sources of Stress

Introduction

As an occupational group, the clergy scored highly in a Cabinet Office survey for job satisfaction. Central to their satisfaction is the meaningfulness of their work.[25] When stress becomes endemic that meaningfulness is weakened and sometimes lost. This characterizes the world of work today and undermines people's efforts to work well. Organizational psychology provides a vocabulary and an objective account of recurring sources of stress there. This is helpful for untangling them from one another and for locating them in the work rather than in conflicting personalities. This could make it easier to discuss work difficulties more dispassionately.

Stress at Work from an Organizational Perspective

Stress at work is not always a problem; it can be energizing and motivating. It is when pressure becomes too much that this changes. The Health and Safety Executive has identified six common ways this happens:

- volume overload;
- lack of appropriate control;
- lack of appropriate support;
- relationships at work;
- role-based stress;
- changes in the job and the organization.[26]

Work Overload

Having too much to do, or unrealistic timeframes in which to do it, results from pressures within and outside the organization, from uncertainty arising from increasing demands or responsibilities, challenging levels of work difficulty, and uneven distribution of resources. Some of these may result from organizational restructuring. There is also 'qualitative overload' when one's skills set is stretched beyond one's competence. This is 'now endemic within the clerical profession.[27] Work overload also distorts someone's work-life balance so that they spend less time in family and social relationships. Consequently, the buffer effect that these social relationships provide is reduced. Managers are particularly at risk in this way.[28]

Lack of Control and Lack of Support

Underlying both these categories is what has been called 'the psychological contract' between those with ultimate control in an organization and those affected by their decisions. This refers to 'the unwritten set of mutual expectations held by organizations and their employees which can play a major role in determining attitudes in the workplace.' Two elements are central here: the sense of fairness and trust and the dynamics of the transaction between employer and employees.[29] Where organizational support is perceived to be reduced, this psychological contract becomes strained.

A serious example of lack of control that breaches this contract is harassment and bullying. This is defined as 'perceiving oneself being on the receiving end of negative actions...where the target has difficulty in defending him or herself against these actions.' Clergy can behave like this but are often at the receiving end of it, too. Either way, such behaviours are both symptoms of, and generators of, stress, for colleagues as well as for subordinates.

Role-based Stress

Parish clergy are particularly exposed to this as they play many roles to many audiences. Taking on a new role is naturally stressful because one has left the familiar but not yet come to terms with the new. Those with mixed feelings about taking on new responsibilities, are most likely to experience stress at the start. (One study reported this among nursing graduates during the first three months of their employment. After a year, it was then overtaken by work overload!) The stress of such transitions has been noted in clergy, particularly in curates and those moving to their first post of responsibility.[30] This is why curates value opportunities for making sense of their experiences so highly and why they appreciate training incumbents who can offer this.[31] The importance of providing such support is indicated by research showing that stress from both role conflict and role ambiguity is greater when employees perceive its lack.

Role Conflict

Roles generate stress when there is a lack of clarity about goals and objectives, resulting in incompatible goals or tasks that are not perceived to be part of one's job. This can lead to a range of negative effects from job dissatisfaction, lack of self-confidence, lowered self-esteem, depression and low work motivation. The fact that ongoing change is endemic now, in various forms, needs to be recognized as a generator of conflict and stress. Examples are:

- moving to a more responsible role, especially early in the career span,
- being confronted with change without adequate preparation,
- organizations demanding more from staff, such as taking more initiatives than they are used to taking, and without providing adequate support.

Change, then, is a significant source of stress and this is intensified by a lack of consultation or adequate training. For example, those at managerial levels experience this when unable to meet others' expectations of their job role. What reduces such stress is introducing changes through an open process of dialogue and discussion. The absence of such preparation and support leads, not surprisingly, to various resistant behaviours.

Ministry: Its Occupational Sources of Stress

For the clergy, the conflicts surface most sharply in the contrast between pastoral and administrative roles. These are often felt to be in conflict with each other. Clergy often claim that this contrast is unique to them but similar tensions exist in business and the creative industries.

Another source of stress in ministry is having to behave as a public figure who visibly represents both the community and the institution of the Church. Ministers have to give up thinking of themselves as private persons. Representing the institution, the minister needs to feel connected to it in order to sustain this role.[32] In community life, this means acting as host, facilitator or leader. These roles enable oversight that builds up the church community, both from the centre and on the frontline. This calls for political and people skills that training for ministry does not provide. Facing the conflicts is made more difficult by the Church's culture which does not encourage addressing difficulties openly. I say more on this in the next section.

Two other sources of work stress are the insensitivity of the work organization and the Church's dysfunctional culture. The resulting chronic and systemic stress reflects ongoing everyday pressures from organizational life. Additionally, care providers are affected by their work, first, because it is emotionally draining and secondly, because their institution and their professional body exert both conscious and unconscious demands through the expectations they have. The negative effect of these is 'intensified by the lack of positive feedback that the ordinary care provider needs to sustain their role in the organization.'[33]

Clergy are often caught between unrealistic expectations from parishioners and 'the insensitivity of institutional systems to the personal pressures that (they) experience.'[34] Such sources of stress are not susceptible to single interventions.

The power of these expectations is so strong that people are sometimes unable to adapt to a change in circumstances. For example, a key lay parishioner was unable to be sympathetic when her incumbent's wife died. Reporting this to his successor, she complained, 'The man just fell completely apart!' This demonstrates a significant obstacle to realizing the *Covenant's* suggestion that congregations provide support to their clergy. Small wonder then that clergy sometimes respond defensively and insensitively to protect themselves.

The Culture of the Church

All institutions and professions naturally have aspirations and therefore expectations of their members. They express these through their distinctive culture and their characteristic ways of doing, and not doing things. These will also be influenced by the larger setting of the country and its traditions. Out of this matrix, institutions develop their own culture. Key influences on the culture are the shared expectations and habitual defences needed to cope with overwhelming demands. These are heightened in the Church by two factors in combination, the high ideals that the Church represents and the way that the Church's marginal social situation creates greater pressures around meeting these. Secondly, boundaries in the Church are much more permeable than in a counselling setting, for example, and since most of the Church's members are volunteers, neither are they constrained by the discipline of work. The most visible example of the Church's defensiveness is its culture of chronic niceness. This demands that one must avoid the negative. Consequently, difficult experiences are split off, only to break out when the niceness can no longer be maintained.[35] There is a high price to be paid for dealing with the negative aspects of experience in this way. It comes out in other ways that feeds a culture of distrust:

- Lack of clarity about roles, expectations, accountability and decision-making
- Challenge of trusting across different traditions and value systems
- Lack of attention to personal and role boundaries, including around confidentiality
- Isolation between individuals and parts of the institution
- Perception that parts of the institution are governed by a managerial rather than a pastoral assumption
- A lack of honesty and openness and a fear of being found out

- The often unconscious impact of feeling like an institution in decline
- …a lack of ability, benevolence, integrity or predictability[36]

This combination of a culture of niceness with dynamics of distrust does not support clergy for dealing with such recurring difficulties of ministry as unhealthy relationship patterns and conflicts that are often underneath the surface.[37]

The fact that clergy are not trained or prepared for these difficulties is one reason they become defensive. We see, then, an interrelated dynamic of difficulties for which clergy (and church members generally) have not been prepared and rigid defences they use to manage them. This defensive pattern pervades the Church as institution. It also encourages immature dependency and distrust.

All this suggests some larger pressure that the institution and its members are needing to defend against. In organizations, having more flexible and appropriate defences depends on how their leaders address the organization's challenges. The shared anxieties behind these defences do not enable Church members to address those realistically. Responses on all sides can oscillate abruptly from being charming to being harsh. The resulting ineffective actions undermine the morale and sense of purpose of the clergy, and of many lay people too. Consequently, behind much stress in ministry, is the experience of the Church as a straitjacket, as Canon Simon Butler described it in General Synod.[38]

Questions for Reflection

- Did this chapter help you to understand the pressures you experience in your community of faith and in workplace outside Church?
- How do you see the 'psychological contract,' between those with ultimate control and those affected, working out in your faith community and/or your ministry?
- In what ways do you find yourself behaving with 'chronic niceness'? How could you act differently?

The Clergy's Experience of Pastoral Care

4

The Need to Reconceive Pastoral Care in Social Terms

Introduction

There is a story about how I chose this topic. As a minister and psychotherapist doing a professional doctorate, I wanted to research a concern from the practice of ministry that could be illuminated by the practice of psychotherapy. For the doctorate, it needed to be a question to which I did not know the answer. Failing to find one, I met up with two colleagues over dinner, hoping they would help me. At first we made no progress and so fell into gossiping. Then we realized that all the stories we had been sharing were examples of clergy behaving badly, by being rude or unhelpful in various ways. One friend, with much experience of training volunteers for organizations like Traidcraft, shed some light on this. 'Such organizations depend on their volunteers and so really have to look after them. The Church is not like that.' This prompted me to ask: so what *is* the clergy's experience of pastoral care? The novelty of this theme was demonstrated by the difficulty people have had in hearing the question. Many could not believe what they heard and said did I not mean the pastoral care ministers provide!

My research was on a small scale and constrained by academic time requirements so it is suggestive rather than comprehensive. Nonetheless, it provides a fresh perspective on the subjects of the stress of ministry, clergy well-being, and pastoral care as the means to provide it. I conducted it with a small, homogeneous focus group of middle-aged men that met four times. From the material I gathered, I shall describe the four most important themes.

These are formation, 'bad experiences of pastoral care,' the limits of the one-to-one model and public speech as a means of pastoral care.

Formation

Identifying formation as an important part of pastoral care reminds us that pastoral care begins as an ordinary part of life from the cradle to the grave, long before any crisis. Exploring it revealed the significance of organizational and institutional factors that are under-appreciated as sources of pastoral care. All the focus group members had come to their vocation through their membership of specific ecclesial communities. Three aspects of their experience were formative: acceptance, legitimacy and redemption or rescue.

All of them had found it hard to join other groups. In their formational communities, they found themselves accepted for who they were in a way that was new. The second theme emerged without prompting from me when one spoke of how important it had been to be somewhere (his college at university) where ordination was 'esteemed and respected.' The others then described comparably affirming experiences. The third theme, of redemption or rescue, emerged when Mark talked about his parents. In his teens, they had many rows which he found very disturbing. When he could no longer bear it, the only place he could think to 'turn to was the vicarage.' He was able to do this because he had experienced the vicar (and, I guess, church members) as different from his parents. He talked of needing 'a world from which to view another world.'

'Bad' Experiences of Pastoral Care

As these emerged in the group discussions, they had a common theme: the senior clergy involved were apparently unable to respond to the needs of the priest in front of them. Either they were more concerned about the church's reputation than for the priest in front of them or they were so trapped within the norm of niceness that they were unable to respond with concern to the particular issue. An example of the first was given by Matthew who had reported that he was having money difficulties. Later 'the bishop called on (him) and spoke in a rather heavy way, asking if it was going to lead to any publicity...' Two others, who had referred to difficulties in their marriages, reported similar responses. One described 'a rather heavy-handed response, which was not particularly helpful,' and which suggested that the senior clergy were mainly concerned to avoid a scandal. He had not 'felt (his) difficulties were that great; I was just responding to the question on the form.' His lasting impression was 'that the concern was not really for him...' The other felt that his incumbent was too embarrassed by the subject to be able to address it with him. These responses reveal how anxiety undermined the ability of senior clergy to support someone with a difficulty or even to try to understand what the nature of it was. I should add that they did also give examples of some good experiences.

Limitations of the One-to-one Model of Support

In a pre-COVID-19 study of trust and trustworthiness in one diocese, clergy talked of their feelings of isolation, the diminishing respect they experienced in the wider community, the spread of fewer clergy across more parishes and all this coupled with heightened expectations and scrutiny on what they deliver in a consumer-led society.[39]

Clearly, these concerns arise from the occupation of ministry. The counselling model is inadequate as a means of support since what is most needed is understanding and affirmation from within the Church organization. Whilst one-to-one support can be very helpful as some archdeacons reported during COVID-19, it is impossible to do this for everyone.[40]

This is why senior clergy push back against the clergy's wishes for more support. This is illustrated by how Yvonne Warren responds to the issue in her book on the state of the clergy, *The Cracked Pot*. As both a marital therapist and the widow of a senior clergyman, she is able to be sympathetic both to the clergy wishing for more support from their seniors and to the seniors who have many heavy responsibilities. However, she struggles sometimes to do justice to the clergy's wish for more support. With her therapeutic sensitivities, she focuses more on personality issues than on the systemic or occupational ones. Then she delegitimizes their wish for more support by ascribing a pathological aspect to it, that they did not have effective fathers and then speaks critically of their 'dependency needs' as immature.[41]

However, there are alternatives to that individual approach as I discovered from other researchers in the caring professions. One needs to change one's focus from the individual to the group and think in social and organizational terms. I shall address this in the final two chapters.

Obstacles to Meeting the Needs of Staff

At the heart of pastoral activity is a meeting of need with response. It needs to be said that turning to someone for support, when one needs it, is healthy dependency in action. The examples of 'bad care' I described showed how anxiety undermined the ability of senior clergy to provide this. Investigating pastoral care through the clergy's own experiences highlights the social character of that anxiety. Two characteristic defences are for managers in the care sector to ignore 'the social, group and psychological aspects of work' and in healthcare settings for staff to locate all the sickness in the patients and all the health in the staff.[42] This disallows the healthy part of the patient and encourages unhealthy forms of either dependency or independence. It also disallows the ill-being of the workers. Something similar is visible in the Church. An organizational culture shaped by such anxieties can lead to the fear of asking for help which is 'a reliable sign of a dysfunctional organization.'[43]

Turning to someone for support, when one needs it, is healthy dependency in action

These examples show how anxiety can distort both sides of the helping relationship and many of the complaints that clergy and people make reflects this. This drives a dysfunctional dynamic, oscillating between exaggerated distancing and closeness. Other examples are the passivity of parishioners that parish clergy lament and the hard to reach character that both senior and frontline clergy lament about each other. From either side of this and other divides, the defensive responses reinforce each other.

Conclusion

From this review of the clergy's experience of pastoral care I direct your attention to two important things. First, to unshrink our understanding of pastoral care we need to include social and organizational resources and particularly the good, ordinary ecclesial community. Secondly, we need to recognize the destructive effects of the Church's culture. The report on *Trust and Trustworthiness* makes this impossible to ignore, reminding us not only of the major breaches of trust that have occurred but also describing ways to repair them. I draw on that in the discussion about how we can care for the Church. Part of that, they say, will be to provide a narrative to take us forward. I shall address both topics in the final two chapters, not with anything like a comprehensive plan but to show the need to close the gap in our thinking and acting between the pastoral and leadership tasks.

Questions for Reflection

- How was your faith community important in your growing in faith?
- Do you now experience your current community as a caring one?
- Are you aware of anxiety affecting how you live out your faith?
- Are you given opportunities to exercise your healthy side, for example, to use your life experience and/or professional skills in the life of the community?

5 Embodying the Church's Essential Task

Introduction

Promoting the well-being of the Church and providing a narrative to take us forward are not usually seen as pastoral care. But both are part of what the New Testament calls oversight. Addressing the Church as a whole and its parts, these two activities reach what individually focused responses miss. Both provide pastoral care, and they share a principle which I call the Church's essential task that is expressed by all who address pastoral issues. I include four different versions.

I develop the first from the definition of pastoral care that has been my reference point. It was distilled by Alastair Campbell from his research into pastoral care in the Christian tradition as 'increasing love between people and between people and God.'[44] It is exemplified by worship. Pursuing this principle involves facing two ways at the same time, towards God on the one hand and towards people and society on the other. This is made more difficult by the loss of that social acceptance of faith that was once fully expressed in Christendom. The decline of that social expression places a question mark against it which generates anxiety. That is why legitimacy was an issue for the members of the focus group and why making sense of things in the light of the gospel is a vital element in pastoral care today. Such anxiety arises from the work of ministry and its setting. Because it is often not addressed, it hinders fulfilling the pastoral task. As a constructive response, I focus on the well-run organization (a good place to work or a good church to belong to) and the value of making meaning through public speech. Both can help to alleviate this anxiety and give people strength to face life's challenges. It is important to recover them as important expressions of pastoral care.

Facing both ways needs a dialogue between the demands of each pole of the dynamic. Ministers often feel pressure from one and go too far toward it. Then they are pulled 'further inside the church and relatively isolated from society or further into society and correspondingly less in touch with the church on the other.'[45]In other words, the temptation is to be 'so heavenly minded that one is no earthly use' or so identified with the setting of one's ministry, one is no pastoral use. For example, the bad examples of pastoral care I have reported showed senior clergy being so organizationally minded that they were unable to respond pastorally. Frontline clergy can be the same.

Worship as Model of the Essential Task

What is involved becomes clearer when we consider the task of leading worship. This is the second version of this principle. It involves taking people through an oscillating process from independence and their everyday functioning to dependence on God and then back to independence and everyday life. People return to that strengthened by their worship of God. Clearly, if one side of the process is omitted, the transformative effects of worship will be lost. The minister's role is to facilitate this process.[46]

To do this, ministers need to be grounded in that pivotal dynamic of facing two ways, toward God and towards society. Doing so brings the transcendent dimension into the ecology of pastoral care. It also requires an ongoing rethinking process that comes to fruition through the interaction between both earthly and heavenly concerns. For example, the well-run church organization, at whatever level, brings the transcendent and the organizational mundane into relationship with each other. This is a gift to the world as the following example demonstrates.

The Essential Task Organizationally

The modern hospice was the brainchild of Cicely Saunders. Because she approached medicine's big issue of death and dying from her perspective of faith, she was led to challenge the prevailing assumptions that medicine meant cure and dying was failure. She showed how medical care could be redirected, in partnership with spiritual care, to help people make a good ending to their lives. Bridging the prevailing split in this way, she produced a new wholeness of practice. The result is the distinctive ethos of hospice care. The *Trust* report calls for the Church to do something similar in response to the Church's ill-being.[47]

Facing the Hard Issues

The big issue facing the Church and its ministers is, symbolically, also about death, namely, the death of the Church that is threatened by decline and its increased pressures on ministry. These generate powerful feelings of loss and helplessness from which people need to defend themselves.

The authors of the *Trust* report identify 'perceived decline' as a factor behind the other hard issue facing the Church, namely, the many breaches of trust and the resulting climate of distrust and suspicion that exists between all parts of the institution. It also exists between the Church and the world, fuelled by the inconsistency between the Church's values and its behaviour, such as abuse of children and failures to act, its long-term racism and how the Church has handled its internal disputes.

The failure here is a spiritual one, an example of losing that pivotal faith-trust connection with God in our organizational behaviour. Rather than accepting the realities of failing or dying, in faithful dependency on the Lord, we as an institution, mesmerized by the numbers charting decline, focus on quantity and action. This would matter less if those representing the pastoral, spiritual or educational strands of the Church's life were not so often excluded from key decision-making. Losing the pivotal connection plays out as one-sidedness organizationally.

The loss of the faith-trust relationship with God is also behind the resistance to allowing others to be dependent on them. The resulting suspicious attitudes reflect that people feel unsupported.[48] The report's call to all in the Church to renew their trust in God in relation to these pressures and questioning arising from decline is timely.

Repairing the Distrust

They write that efforts to repair the distrust need to be shaped by this two-way dynamic too, for example, by 'scrutiny of the culture and structure of ministry that allowed this to happen *combined with* study and reflection on Christian teaching and practice of trust.' Specifically, on 'the obligations' that flow from God's gifts to us, including 'repentance and forgiveness.' The report provides suggestive examples from research into those 'employers who best maintained trust' during the COVID-19 pandemic. However, following these will be dependent on coming to terms with the realities of decline and the various breaches of trust. This will be hard for a Church that is so divided and mutually suspicious.

Reversing the Dynamics of Distrust in the Church

That research, from which the report draws, highlights the importance of leaders knowing and agreeing among themselves what their organization stands for, and having a sense of personal integrity and a shared sense of the right thing to do.[49] This requires a willingness to turn one's scrutiny upon oneself, something that people with power can easily avoid. As another interesting paper on the perils of leadership declares, 'power is a mind-altering drug.'[50]

Finally, I flag-up a suggestive approach from practitioners who know from the inside about the difficult dynamics in the health service. It was developed in response to the recent scandals of abusive care in some hospitals. Based on the idea of intelligent kindness, it shows what giving attention means in practice. It has its version of the two-way relationship, expressed through 'kinship (on one side) and working for the common good (on the other.' This generative process then focuses on 'kindness which leads to attentiveness, a noticing that increases understanding. This generates attunement and warm engagement. The point is that trust results from being recognized and this leads to good collaboration which leads to well-being and satisfaction.[51] In the call to repair how we relate across organizational boundaries this shows the steps involved in introducing the kindness of personal relationships into our organizational ones.

Question for Reflection

- Does the principle of 'the Church's essential task' help you to see and make sense of Church life differently?
- How could you and your community do things differently in the light of worship and the hospice as models?
- Thinking about the faith-trust connection with God, does that influence your behaviour, as a Church member or office holder, in the same way as it does your personal life?

Speaking the Church's Essential Task

6

Public Speech as Pastoral Care

At a friend's licensing service, I sat up when the bishop addressed the subject of expectations. He commented that from their parish profile it was clear they all had 'very high expectations of David,' their new vicar. Looking at them, he raised his eyebrow questioningly, paused, and then moved on to something else. That is when I saw the missed opportunity.

The bishop could have addressed this widespread issue by speaking publicly of how our hopes and expectations run ahead of what we can realistically achieve. This could have helpfully prepared people for when disappointment arose. For example, one could reframe these expectations as visionary hopes that give a sense of purpose and direction, but which should not be taken literally. Developing this theme could also help loosen the grip of the norm of niceness by showing people how to be hopeful in truthful and pragmatic language. A sermon could then be an expression of social pastoral care and a way of making meaning. This is another significant way to mediate between God and society. These opportunities already exist; what is needed is the intention and preparation to use them to good effect.

The *Trust* report gives necessity and urgency to this. Facing difficult situations and especially crises, the employers who best maintained trust among their employees were those who provided bridging narratives connecting the past to the future, showing how their organization's meaning and purpose could survive. Promoting a shared sense of belonging and purpose is the institution's role.[52]

Public Speech as Straddling the Boundary

However, using meaningful public speech in this way is not usual in Church life. Consequently, significant pastoral need is not being met on the very occasions when clergy might reasonably expect that it would be. This was confirmed for me when I shared my thinking with one senior clergy person whom I did not know well. Would he be sympathetic to my claim for the pastoral opportunity of public speech? After I spoke, there was quite a pause. Then, slowly, he spoke. 'Every year, at the Chrism service, I see the hungry look on the faces of the clergy as the bishop starts to speak. And at the end, I see the disappointment on their faces.' That confirmed for me that real pastoral need is going unmet. This gives fresh urgency to this task of making meaning publicly.

However, I also want to acknowledge how difficult a task this is. Much public life is dominated by two forms of language that blank out meaning making. These are the languages of bureaucracy and administration and those of advertising and consumerism, and that includes the soundbites politicians use in place of argument. We do not have many models of people making meaning in public speech. Again, it needs that capacity to face both ways I described in the last chapter and that depends on personally wrestling with the issues and being willing to put oneself in the frame.

Evading this, not least because of the pressure of many demands, has become a cultural norm within the Church so that it takes a serious, intentional commitment to make time for that necessary preparation. This includes ongoing homework, of prayer, reading and reflection, to be able to address this hunger for spiritual nourishment and encouragement today and to do so in an interesting and intelligent way.

Facing two ways in public speech within and between groups is a challenging opportunity. There is the possibility of saying something meaningful, from our vision of the kingdom of God, about how or why the Church functions as it does and finally, about how and why people and their travails matter. When clergy fall back on clichés they reinforce the sense that the Church does not have something to contribute. This is hardly helpful. I shall describe how I think about these opportunities in terms of three elements, enfolded together: presence, making sense and encounter.

Presence

If that first bishop had stayed with the issue of unrealistic expectations sympathetically, and if the second could have spoken in a way that fed the clergy, each would have made themselves more present to their listeners. That would have reduced the gap between the centre and those on the front line. That is how presence matters. It is a willingness to be present with the difficulties without necessarily knowing the answers or being able to provide what people are wanting. This is particularly important in relation to the anger and disappointment many feel and want to express and leads to the next point.

Making Sense

Making sense follows naturally from this. First, showing one has understood and then exploring what this might mean. After all, interpreting is fundamental to human life and vital to ministry. It begins when the mother helps the child to make sense of both their inward and outer experiences of the world and other people. By doing this, she 'becomes a point of reality, *an interpreter of what the child experiences so that it becomes a liveable whole'* (my italics). This is different from knowing facts or traditional formulations. In our fact-saturated culture it is tempting to abandon making sense in order to multiply our random knowing. But motherhood, (for which read pastoral care) is about 'making sense.'[53] This is obligatory because so many issues trouble both clergy and people. It was an issue that came up in Warren's research, of troubled clergy wishing their seniors would help them make sense of these. I suspect the people have similar wishes of their clergy.[54]

Encounter

This combination of presence and interpretation opens up a space of encounter and exploration in which people discover the who and the what that is beyond them and the facts they know. At its best, such speech facilitates 'a moment when things blossom into meaning.'[55] This opens up new possibilities and transforms their understanding. We are familiar with enabling this on an individual level. We need to learn how to do this together in and for groups as well.

The Demands of Making Sense in Practice

This calls for an institutional *metanoia,* an intentional turning away from the protective safety of saying as little as possible towards more open and honest speech. The obstacles to this are huge and the *Trust* report sees them as characteristic of the Church's institutional life. I suggested in the last chapter, that such embedded defensiveness reflects the anxieties of the institution in its current context.

This three-cornered model, of presence, interpretation and encounter, is another way of expressing that pivotal relationship of faith in ministry. It is a way for us to face our own version of the anxieties as well as a way to speak pastorally. Facing the dark moments of ministry, when we are most afraid or feeling a failure is also, as we know of course, the way to rediscover God and to recover trust. The clergy's longing for support is that their senior clergy play a part in this three-cornered process, by offering them what they endeavour to offer to their parishioners. When it does not happen, it gives clergy good reasons for retreating into isolation and congregations likewise. We can start to undo this by taking small steps to be present where we are, seeking understanding by attending and listening and being open to encounter, especially with those we find difficult.

The Significance of Care and the Role of Oversight

Finally, taking care how we relate in our organizational roles matters. It can release energy. It is not characteristic of managers and it is hard to sustain under pressure.[56] There is a prophetic opportunity to make the provision of pastoral care a witness to the gospel because…

> The ability to care is the hallmark of the human, the touchstone of morality and the ground of holiness. Without the warmth of care, the world becomes a graveyard. In the kindness of care, the divine comes alive in us.[57]

Both the clergy's capacity for this and the vitality of local ecclesial communities depend in some measure on their receiving the pastoral care of good oversight. This is highly relevant to efforts to renew the Church because in the end:

> It is the actual praxis, that is, the life and thought of Christian communities, which will decide the future of Christianity in this world. Only if the Christian faith is lived today and if the centre of that is the presence of God in Christ in all our lives and is experienced today… will authentic Christianity continue.[58]

Notes

1 H Sherwood, 'Being parish priest was my most stressful job, says Justin Welby,' *The Guardian*, 10 July 2017.

2 *Covenant for Clergy Care and Wellbeing*, GS 2133.

3 K Burgess and R Watts, survey of Church of England clergy, *The Times*, 30 August 2023. Living Ministry Survey: 2017: https://www.churchofengland.org/sites/default/files/2017-10/Living_Ministry_Panel_Survey_Wave_1_Report.pdf. Unite finds faith workers bearing the brunt of the cost-of-living crisis, *Church Times*, 23 October 2023.

4 'Number of ordinands has plummeted,' *Church Times*, 12 July 2024.

5 *Trust and Trustworthiness within the Church of England—a Preliminary Report*, GS 2354.

6 'Six ways to thrive,' *Church Times*, 15 January 2021.

7 I owe the term 'ill-being' to a personal communication from John Ballat.

8 A V Campbell, 'Pastoral Care, the Nature of' in A V Campbell (ed), *A Dictionary of Pastoral Care* (London: SPCK, 1987).

9 D F Ford, *The Shape of Living* (Norwich: Canterbury Press Books, 2012) p 103.

10 C Maslach, *Burnout: The Cost of Caring* (Cambridge, MA: Maior Books, 2003).

11 J M Kouzes and B Z Posner, *Credibility* (San Francisco, CA: Jossey-Bass Publishers, 1993).

12 C Lee and S Horsman, *Affirmation and Accountability* (Sheldon: Society of Mary and Martha, 2002).

13 J Davey, *Burnout: Stress in the Ministry* (Leominster: Gracewing, 1995).

14 S Pattison, *Pastoral Care and Liberation Theology* (London: SCM Press, 1997).

15 T Oden, *Care of Souls in the Classic Tradition* (Minneapolis, MN: Fortress Press, 1984).

16 A V Campbell, *A Dictionary of Pastoral Care, op cit.*

17 J Davey, *Burnout: Stress in the Ministry, op cit.*

18 D W Hardy, *Finding the Church* (London: SCM Press, 2001) p 23.

19 A Weinberg, V J Sutherland and C Cooper, *Organizational Stress Management* (Basingstoke: Palgrave Cooper, 2010).

20 'Happiness and Work: An Interview with Lord Richard Layard,' 1 July 2019, McKinsey and Company. Interview with Tera Allas, director of research and economics at the McKinsey Centre for Government: accessed 7 January 2024.

21 C Black, *Working for a Healthier Tomorrow: Dame Carol Black's Review of the Health of Britain's Working Age Population* (London: The Stationery Office, 2008).

22 B R Wilson, *Religion in Secular Society* (London: C A Watts, 1966) cited in A Russell, *The Clerical Profession* (London: SPCK, 1980).

23 D Browning (1974).

24 A Russell, *The Clerical Profession, op cit.*

25 M Easton, 'Vicar or Publican—Which Jobs Make You Happy?' BBC News (www.bbc.co.uk/news/magazine-26671221): accessed 8 January 2024.

26 'Work-related Stress and How to Manage It,' Health and Safety Executive, 2006: https://www.hse.gov.uk/stress/overview.htm: accessed 8 January 2024.

27 Gallup Clergy Survey 1986 (commissioned by the Archbishop of Canterbury's Commission on Urban Priority Areas).

28 A Weinberg, V J Sutherland and C Cooper, *Organizational Stress Management, op cit.* This chapter is based on the above except when other sources are cited.

29 *ibid.*

30 'Collaborative Ministry and Transitions to First Incumbency,' Living Ministry Focussed Study 1: https://www.churchofengland.org/sites/default/files/2021-05/living-ministry-collaborative-ministry-report.pdf

31 E Miller, 'A Church of England' in *From Dependency to Autonomy: Studies in Organization and Change* (London: Free Association Books, 1993) and personal communication from the Revd Dr Greg Smith.

32 A Dartington, 'Where Angels Fear to Tread: Idealism, Despondency and Opportunities for Thought in Hospital Nursing' in A Obholzer and V Zagier Roberts (eds), *The Unconscious at Work* (London: Routledge, 1994).

33 Lee and Horsman, *Affirmation and Accountability, op cit.*

34 Maslach, *Burnout, op cit.*

35 P Speck, 1994, 'Working with Dying People: On Being Good Enough' in A Obholzer and V Zagier Roberts, *The Unconscious at Work, op cit.*

36 I compiled this list from these two sources: C Lee and S Horsman, *Affirmation and Accountability, op cit; Trust and Trustworthiness within the Church of England, op cit.*

37 S Savage, 'On the analyst's couch' in S Croft, *The Future of the Parish System* (London: Church House Publishing, 2006) pp 22–24.

38 'Causes of clergy stress aired in the General Synod' in *Church Times*, 09 July 2017.

39 *Trust and Trustworthiness within the Church of England, op cit.*

40 Personal communication, the Ven Derek Chezey.

41 Y Warren, *The Cracked Pot: The State of Today's Anglican Clergy* (Stowmarket: Kevin Mayhew, 2002).

42 A Obholzer and V Zagier Roberts, *The Unconscious at Work, op cit.* T Main, 'The Hospital as a Therapeutic Institution' in *The Ailment and other Psychoanalytic Essays* (London: Free Association Books, 1989).

43 R Sennett, *Respect* (London: Penguin, 2003) p 119.

44 A V Campbell (ed), *A Dictionary of Pastoral Care, op cit.*

45 E Miller, 'A Church of England' in *From Dependency to Autonomy: Studies in Organization and Change, op cit.*

46 B Reed, *The Dynamics of Religion* (London: Darton, Longman and Todd, 1978) p 174.

47 *Trust and Trustworthiness within the Church of England, op cit.*

48 K Burgess and R Watts, *The Times, op cit.*

49 V H Hailey and K Jacobs, 'Responsible Business in Crisis' (London: CIPD): https://www.cipd.org/uk/knowledge/reports/responsible-business-through-crisis/ cited in *Trust and Trustworthiness within the Church of England, op cit.*

50 R Turner and J Gosling, 'Expert Viewpoint: Character, Company and Context. A Practical Framework for Leaders under Pressure,' *Colombo Business Journal*, 14 (1), 2023, 19–42.

51 P Campling and J Ballat, *Intelligent Kindness: Reforming the Culture of Health Care* (RCPsych Publications, 2011). A short introduction to their thinking is available here: https://www.researchgate.net/figure/ntelligent-kindness-a-virtuous-circle_fig1_272409469

52 V H Hailey and K Jacobs, 'Responsible Business in Crisis,' *op cit.*

53 M Furlong, *Travelling In* (London: Hodder and Stoughton, 1971).

54 Y Warren, *The Cracked Pot, op cit.*

55 C Ernst, *Multiple Echo: Explorations in Theology* (London: Darton, Longman and Todd, 1979).

56 P Lencioni, *The Advantage* (San Francisco, CA: Jossey Bass, 2012).

57 J O'Donohue, *Divine Beauty: The Invisible Embrace* (London: Bantam Edition, 2004).

58 W Jeanrond, *Text and Interpretation: As Categories of Theological Thinking* (Dublin: Gill and Macmillan, 1987).